EDUCATOR SELF-CARE

First paperback edition April 2022

Design by Alana Bowman
Edited by Marcela P. Cartagena

Print ISBN: 978-1737690603

Published by Tapir Educational Press

Dedicated to all the educators with whom we have worked over the years. Without their honesty and willingness to share their professional and personal experiences and struggles, I would not have this list of self-care strategies that are shared in this book.

Table of Contents

A tremendous thank you to the TREP Project staff who worked on developing many of the resources shared in this book. Thank you, Jamilah Bowden, Jessica Nixon, and Stacy Williams, for your dedication and passion for developing resources for educators. Thank you, Alexandra Ehrhardt, Ebony Hinton, Hilary Tackie, and Nick Wilkins, for your support in developing the resources. I'd like to also thank Kat Edmiston and Pranathi Posa for editing early drafts of the graphic organizers.

Introduction

Education is an emotionally demanding profession with ever-increasing expectations, but being an educator is profoundly rewarding, which is why many educators "push through" when they feel overwhelmed.However, pushing through can bring negative consequences for you and your students. It's not good for you or your students to believe that you should ignore your needs because "that's the job we signed up for."

Experiencing high levels of stress over long periods of time without adequate coping resources will negatively impact your wellbeing and your students' success. To ensure that you can have a long career, it's important that you learn to recognize when your stress levels are elevated and then engage in self-care.

Self-care is about taking deliberate action to restore and improve health and wellbeing. It's a powerful tool for preventing, managing, and recovering from stress and its damaging consequences. Whenever possible, use strategies that you can integrate into your daily routines.

Self-care is directing the care that you give to others towards yourself through self-compassion. This includes acknowledging that everyone in life, including yourself, has challenges, is imperfect, and can't meet all your students' needs. Practicing self-compassion is especially important for educators working in schools serving large numbers of students coping with trauma.

Self-care is not indulgence nor a sign of weakness; it's essential for balancing the natural costs of caring about and for those more vulnerable than ourselves. Educators are especially vulnerable to feelings of anxiety and emotional distress, becoming mentally and emotionally worn out, and feeling overwhelmed by their students' traumas.

Think of self-care as taking...

Time to do less for a moment so that you can better address your tasks and responsibilities	*Time to connect with yourself to then be able to share more of yourself with students*	*Time to clear your mind and assess your values to create a rewarding and sustainable career*

The truth is, you already know that self-care is necessary for your longevity as an educator; it's just that you haven't been able to prioritize it. This book is for you to reflect, read and re-read and put into action to prevent, manage, and heal from the psychologically, emotionally, and physically demanding job of being an educator. You can't give your students the care and compassion that you can't give to yourself—at least not for very long.

Negative Effects of Professional Stress

Educator burnout has severe implications for schools and the broader education system. High educator turnover contributes to significant declines in student achievement, substantial investment losses, and destabilization of schools in highly disadvantaged neighborhoods.

Extended exposure to extreme stress can cause emotional exhaustion, social detachment, heightened senses of fear, anxiety, helplessness, and estrangement from work. Excessive stress can also disrupt how you process and respond to information and experiences, and it can exacerbate a range of physical and psychological ailments.

Decreased professional capacity along with increased risk of compassion fatigue and burnout can severely impair the success of students. After all, educators in these circumstances are less perceptive of and responsive to students' needs.

As many throughout history have noted, time is fluid and flexible—we make time for the experiences we prioritize. This means that your lack of engaging in self-care is less about not having enough time and more about how you prioritize the importance of claiming time for self-care in your professional and personal life. This workbook is an invitation for you to claim time for attending to and restoring your wellbeing.

Here are some broad guidelines to support you on your sustainable self-care journey. Engaging in self-care allows you to reflect on your emotional, financial, and physical needs, nurture relationships in work and non-work areas of your life, and maintain balance and boundaries between work and personal life.

ASSESS
Start with building awareness of the aspects of your life that are out of balance.

Reflect: How do you currently cope with stress and practice self-care?

Begin with the Self-Care Graphic Organizer titled *Plan for Success* to get a sense of the current status of your engagement with self-care. Then complete the Self-Care Graphic Organizer titled *Overcoming Self-Care Obstacles* to address potential barriers to improving your self-care practices.

PLAN
Identify ways to respond to the aspects of your wellbeing that need more attention.

Add and subtract: What practices do you want to incorporate into your self-care plan?

Complete Self-Care Graphic Organizer titled *Forming Healthy Habits* to determine whether and how to incorporate new self-care strategies into your work and home routines. The worksheet also prompts you to think about how you'll overcome potential obstacles in implementing your plan.

TAKE ACTION
Move the plan into action with feasible strategies.

Share and follow-through: How will you hold yourself accountable to your plan?

Complete the Self-Care Graphic Organizer titled *Scheduling Self-Care* to add self-care to your calendar. Making an initial commitment to self-care is great, but it takes continued effort to maintain it. Consider sharing some of your plans with people you trust, including friends, family, partners, and colleagues, who can act as sources of support and help hold you accountable.

ANALYZE AND ADJUST
Adapt based on assessments of your successes and challenges.

Reflect: How will you ensure that you can continue to practice self-care?

The only constant is change, so keep track of how your plan is going and make changes as needed. Complete the Self-Care Graphic Organizer titled *Reflecting on Self-Care* to track your successes and challenges to maintain your motivation and recognizing when revisions and/or support are needed.

There will be times when you will need to lean on others for your self-care. Plan ahead before you are faced with and feel overwhelmed by intense stressors. Complete the Self-Care Graphic Organizer titled *Creating Communities of Care* to help ensure that you will have the social support needed in times of distress.

If Nothing Else, Engage In Mindful Self-Care

This workbook was initially developed during the first eight months of the COVID-19 pandemic when it was critical to focus on self-care practices that can be integrated into educators' everyday lives. The pandemic greatly intensified two intersecting strains of *compassion fatigue* (the emotional strain of providing support to others suffering from traumatic experiences), and *stress-based burnout* (the overwhelming set of expectations and responsibilities at work and at home).

Mindful self-care is an everyday practice that is supported by research showing that it's an effective and sustainable strategy for buffering against compassion fatigue and burnout.

Mindful self-care focuses on using your breath to pause and center yourself in the present moment and to push out regrets of the past and worries of the future.

Allow yourself to connect with your thoughts, feelings, and body without any judgment by simply taking a full, deep breath to initiate one minute of calming self-silence.

You don't need a special space to do this. You can ground yourself in the present moment wherever you are. You can do this while sitting at your desk. You can get up and walk around taking deep breaths with each slow step. You can stand still, or you can stretch.

Over time, regular engagement with brief moments of mindfulness can increase your ability to regulate your emotions and tolerate emotional strains and extend your ability to manage professional and personal frustrations.

There is no time like the present, so begin now. These beginning actions are based on an exercise adapted from The Foundation for a Mindful Society:

- **Set aside some time to begin**, all you need is a few moments of time and some space—it doesn't even need to be a quite space. You just need to quiet yourself in whatever space you are in.

- **Observe the present moment**, including your thoughts, feelings, and body sensations. You are not trying to achieve a state of meditative calm. You are paying attention to and accepting the present moment for what it is.

- **Notice and release your judgments** by accepting all your thoughts, feelings, and sensations as being neither good nor bad, but simply as part of your human experience.

- **Actively engage in self-compassion** by not judging your wandering mind. When you notice your mind wandering, gently return, again and again, to the present moment.

Slow down and give yourself
a moment of calm.

Plan for Success

There are at least five domains of self-care that contribute to our overall wellbeing. It's essential to find balance in each of these domains to maintain your overall health and wellbeing.

Physical wellbeing is affected by your daily habits, such as what you eat, how much you exercise, and how much sleep you get.

Emotional and psychological wellbeing is affected by how you think and feel about yourself and your daily life and by how you cope with life's stressors.

Intellectual wellbeing is affected by activities that stimulate your thinking. These can be related to your profession or other outside interests, such as learning a new skill.

Social wellbeing is affected by your relationships with others, such as the time you spend with friends and the energy you put into maintaining those relationships.

Financial wellbeing is affected by your opportunities and habits concerning earning, saving, and spending.

Self-Care Activities for Each Domain

Physical	Emotional and psychological	Intellectual	Social	Financial
Cook a healthy meal	**Spend** time in nature	**Learn** a new skill	**Call** a friend you haven't talked to in a while	**Start** a savings account
Go for a walk	**Practice** mindfulness	**Update** your resume	**Maintain** relationships that "fill your bucket"	**Make** a budget and stick to it
Drink more water	**Eliminate** toxic social media	**Volunteer** to lead a project at work	**Set** boundaries	**Get** rid of debt
Visit your doctor regularly	**See** a therapist	**Lend** your skills to a community project	**Volunteer** in your community	**Set** financial goals such as buying a home, opening up a retirement account, etc.
Meal-prep for the week	**Take** a "tech break"	**Read** a book	**Expand** your network	**Sell** things you no longer use
Exercise	**Keep** a journal	**Set** professional goals regularly	Double up: **Practice** self-care with a friend!	
Get plenty of sleep	**Use** positive self-affirmations	**Make** a vision board		
Practice taking a break from tech	**Buy** yourself flowers	**Sign** up for a class		
Use your available sick leave at work	**Donate** old clothes			

Begin by reflecting on your current practices and take a moment to list the self-care practices that you are regularly doing. Use the table on the previous page to help you identify these activities.

My Current Self-Care Practices Are...

Physical	Emotional and Psychological	Intellectual	Social	Financial

Reflect on your current practices. Are there domains where you need to practice more self-care?

My Current Self-Care Practices Are...

(leave this page blank to make more copies as needed)

Physical	Emotional and Psychological	Intellectual	Social	Financial

Reflect on your current practices. Are there domains where you need to practice more self-care?

Manage anxiety by using your breath to center yourself in the present moment.

*Slowly breathe in calm.
Slowly breathe out anxiety.*

Overcoming Self-Care Obstacles

To ensure a successful journey to self-care, it's crucial to anticipate obstacles that may come along the way and plan ahead to make sure these hurdles don't hold back your progress.

Take another look at the list of self-care activities on Page 7. List some activities that you would like to add to your self-care practices. Then, list the obstacles keeping you from practicing each activity. Finally, write down at least one way to overcome each obstacle.

New Self-Care Practice	Obstacles to Practice	Possible Solution
I want to start taking a walk during my lunch break.	*I am not walking because I am using my lunch break to catch up on grading.*	*I could ask a parent volunteer to help with grading so I can take a walk.*

Overcoming Self-Care Obstacles

(leave this page blank to make more copies as needed)

New Self-Care Practice	Obstacles to Practice	Possible Solution
I want to start taking a walk during my lunch break.	*I am not walking because I am using my lunch break to catch up on grading.*	*I could ask a parent volunteer to help with grading so I can take a walk.*

In a world of chaos
find your stillness
in your breath.

Start Your Day with Self-Care

There are many reasons why your efforts at self-care may fall short, including infrequent practice (*E.g., "I went for a jog. Why am I not feeling better?"*) and not prioritizing self-care on your long to-do list (*"I'll get to self-care once I'm done folding the laundry"*). Incorporating self-care into your morning routine will help ensure that you are practicing self-care more consistently.

Choose one or two activities from the table below to incorporate into your weekday morning routine or jot down some ideas of your own (this can include things you are already doing). If you find yourself rushed in the morning, select activities that you can get done in little time, such as drinking a glass of water or listening to music as you get ready. Being able to complete the activities consistently is the most important part of building healthy self-care habits.

Physical Self-Care	Social and Emotional Self-Care	Additional Ideas
Do yoga or stretch	Meditate	
Walk or jog	Write in a journal	
Do other type of exercise	Set goals for the day	
Drink a large glass of water	Have coffee with a friend	
Eat a healthy breakfast	Tidy up	
Take a hot bath or shower	Read	
Turn off electronic devices	Practice gratitude	
Spend time outdoors	Listen to relaxing music	

Now, list the one or two self-care activities that you will incorporate into your morning routine:

Activity	Monday	Tuesday	Wednesday	Thursday	Friday
Wake up feeling rested					
Leave for work feeling calm					

In your *breath* there is *power.* Pause and breathe deeply.

End Your Day with Self-Care

As discussed, incorporating self-care into your daily routines will help ensure that you are practicing self-care consistently.

Select one or two activities from the table below to incorporate into your weekday evening routine or jot down some ideas of your own (this can include things you are already doing). If you find yourself rushed or multi-tasking in the evening, choose activities that you can do in little time, such as listening to music while cooking dinner or having "unplugged" time before going to bed. Completing these activities consistently is the key to building healthy self-care habits.

Physical Self-Care	Social and Emotional Self-Care	Additional Ideas
Do yoga or stretch	Meditate	
Walk or jog	Write in a journal	
Do other type of exercise	Set goals for tomorrow	
Drink a large glass of water	Tidy up	
Eat a healthy dinner	Read	
Take a hot bath or shower	Practice gratitude	
Turn off electronic devices	Listen to relaxing music	

Now, list the one or two self-care activities that you will incorporate into your evening routine:

Activity	Monday	Tuesday	Wednesday	Thursday	Friday
Go to sleep feeling calm					

Start and End Your Day With Self-Care

(leave this page blank to make more copies as needed)

List one or two self-care activities that you will incorporate into your **morning routine**:

Activity	Monday	Tuesday	Wednesday	Thursday	Friday
Wake up feeling rested					
Leave for work feeling calm					

List the one or two self-care activities that you will incorporate into your **evening routine**:

Activity	Monday	Tuesday	Wednesday	Thursday	Friday
Go to sleep feeling calm					

Pause wherever you are and whatever you are doing.

Breathe deeply...and *make an intentional decision about what to do next.*

Forming Healthy Habits

Have you ever heard that it takes 21 days to start a new habit and stick to it? It turns out that this is not true. Creating and sustaining healthy habits take constant work and commitment, even after the 21-day mark.

Internationally-acclaimed business coach Tom Bartow created a method for instilling healthier habits in our lives. Use this method to successfully start and maintain good habits. It includes three phases, each with specific steps: the honeymoon phase, the fight through phase, and the second nature phase.

Begin by making your commitment: Pick one self-care practice that you want to become a regular habit. Begin with something simple and easy to stick with, like turning off electronics one hour before going to bed. If you already have a good base of self-care practices, choose something more ambitious like prepping meals for the week on Sunday or stepping up your exercise regimen.

My Healthy Habit Plan

Make the Commitment	*The only way to make a change is to begin to change.* Today I commit to: _____ _____ _____ This is important to me because: _____ _____ _____
Phase 1: The Honeymoon	*This is when you'll be the most excited about starting your habit. As you work to maintain your routine, it's crucial to remind yourself of what motivated you to start.* What inspired you to start your new habit? _____ _____ _____ How will this new habit improve your overall wellbeing? _____ _____ _____ How do you feel when you practice your new habit? _____ _____ _____

My Healthy Habit Plan Continued

Phase 2: The Fight Through

When you begin to lose motivation to maintain your new habit and falling into old routines seems easier, you are in the fight through phase. These strategies will help you fight through and conquer this phase.

Recognize: Say to yourself: ***"I have entered the fight-through phase. I need to push through to win this."*** Continue to give yourself positive self-affirmations as you fight the temptation to give up.

Self-motivate: How will you feel if you stick with this? _____
_____
_____

How will you feel if you don't stick with this? _____
_____
_____

Life projection: What will your life would be like in five years if you don't maintain healthy habits? _____
_____
_____

Phase 3: Second Nature

As your habit begins to become second nature, it may seem like you no longer need to work at maintaining it. However, there are three interruptions to plan for to prevent being thrown back into the fight-through phase.

The discouragement monster: Write yourself an affirmation for when you begin to feel discouraged if your new habit is not producing the results you expected.

Disruptions: What is one thing that may disrupt your new habit, such as a vacation or change in your daily schedule? _____
_____
_____

What is one way that you can continue with your habit, even if in a modified form, through this disruption? _____
_____
_____

Seduction of success: Positive results come from hard work. When you start to see these results, resist the temptation to cut corners.

Breathe deeply and **be** *in the present moment.*

Scheduling Self-Care

Most of us understand that self-care should be a priority in our overall wellness, but making it a priority on our over-packed schedules is often easier said than done. If you schedule self-care the same way you would arrange a meeting or an appointment, you are making sure this time is protected and you will be more likely to practice it.

Monthly Self-Care

Let's look forward to the next month when you may have some openings in your calendar. As you make your schedule for next month, try scheduling a few of the following (or similar) activities. While you may find it challenging to fit in time for self-care every day, this will ensure that you maintain blocks of time for yourself throughout the month.

Now, pick one of these practices and use the repeating events calendar function to add it to your calendar for the next six months.

Weekly Self-Care

What about adding one or two self-care practices that can become a regular part of each week? This could be blocking 30 minutes every Sunday to call a family member or friend who brings you joy. It could also be blocking an hour for that hobby that you've been meaning to enjoy doing again.

Pick one or two days of the week and use the table below to write down one thing that could become a regular part of your self-care routine.

Select day of the week: Monday / Tuesday / Wednesday / Thursday / Friday / Saturday / Sunday
Self-care practice: _____   _____   _____   _____
Select day of the week: Monday / Tuesday / Wednesday / Thursday / Friday / Saturday / Sunday
Self-care practice: _____   _____   _____   _____

Daily Self-Care

Let's make one final push and think about one thing that you can do every day that would enable you to have a moment of daily self-care. Because you will be doing it each day, it should be small and fit within your regular routine. This can be as simple as pausing to take a few breaths to remind yourself that your wellbeing matters in the midst of all that needs to be done for others. To ensure that your commitment happens daily, you need an external reminder to trigger self-care. It can be something that you do as soon as you open your eyes in the morning or when you take a shower or bath. It can also be something that you do at the start or end of your prep period, or just after the final bell for the school day rings.

Every day I will give myself a moment of self-care by _____

_____

_____

_____

_____

More daily self-care ideas:
- Morning or evening gratitude practice.
- Listen to a mindfulness recording before getting out of bed in the morning.
- Take the first 5 minutes of your prep period for a brisk walk outside to clear your mind.
- Stay connected through quick social games like *Words With Friends*.
- Use aromatherapy candles or diffusers to bring a calming scent into your workplace.
- Listen to music during your prep period, get headphones if needed.

Now, reflect back on your monthly, weekly, and daily self-care commitments. What changes do you need to make in order to ensure you have protected time for self-care? _____

_____

_____

_____

_____

_____

_____

_____

_____

_____

_____

_____

Breathe deeply and let go of one thing over which you have no control.

Reflecting on Self-Care

When trying to learn a new skill or improve some aspect of your lifestyle, it's essential to take time for self-reflection. As Jennifer Porter, an executive coach, noted: *"**Reflection** gives the brain an opportunity to pause amidst the chaos, untangle and sort through observations and experiences... and create meaning. This meaning ... can then inform future mindsets and actions."*

To strengthen self-care, we must closely examine how our daily actions and decisions affect our overall health and productivity. As we reflect, we'll learn new skills that will develop into healthy habits and a mindset that will improve all aspects of our lives. This won't happen overnight; but lasting change will come with continued practice and reflection.

Begin by reflecting over the objectives of the Self-Care Graphic Organizers that you have completed thus far. Think about what you planned to do versus what you were actually able to get done. It's OK if you weren't able to complete your plan. Giving yourself grace is part of self-care.

First, take a moment and be grateful for the activities you completed.

What I Planned to Do	What I Actually Did

Now, **reflect on the activities that you were _not_ able to complete** and fill out the table below.

Uncompleted Self-Care Activities	What didn't go as planned?	What can I do to make it work?

Reflecting on Self-Care
(leave this page blank to make more copies as needed)

What are the self-care activities that you...

What I Planned to Do	What I Actually Did

Reflect on the activities that you were not able to complete and fill out the table below:

Uncompleted Self-Care Activities	What didn't go as planned?	What can I do to make it work?

Breathe deeply and
notice the present
as it is
for what it is.

Finding Balance by Setting Priorities

When you are juggling many expectations in different areas of your life and your to-do list is piling up with many uncompleted tasks, deciding what to focus on can be overwhelming. Gain control by setting priorities to achieve balance.

Let's start by listing all of the outstanding tasks you have on your to-do list: both written and in your head. For now, don't try to prioritize any one task over another. No task is too big or too small for this list. Use a separate sheet of paper if you need more space. The goal is to get all of it out of your head and on paper. ***Don't overthink it, just write.***

Stress List of Outstanding Tasks

Work Life	Social Life	Home Life

Now, let's select and prioritize the most important tasks.

A *priority* is something that you set as being more essential over other interests, desires, or concerns. It's important to establish priorities to better manage your time and stay focused on what matters most.

When prioritizing your to-do list, ask yourself the following questions:

Which of these tasks will help me reach my larger life goals? _____

_____

_____

Which of these tasks fulfill me? _____

_____

_____

Which of these tasks are essential to my wellbeing? _____

_____

_____

Example Priorities

Work Life	Social Life	Home Life
Sign up to volunteer my skills with neighborhood task force.	*Schedule the next few video calls with my friends.*	*Use my cookbook planner to make healthier meals.*
Reach back out to the two colleagues that need a mentor.	*Sign up for the next biking club meet-up to meet new people.*	*Stop everything to read to my daughter at bedtime nightly.*
Register for the course I've been wanting to take.	*Return the group emails from my college roommates.*	*Spend time alone, to recharge.*

Now, take a moment to look at your list of tasks from the previous page and write some priorities for yourself. Priorities help you set boundaries for your time and energy. Clear priorities help you say yes to things that promote growth and no to the things that don't.

Before setting your priorities, it's important to remember that we all have **necessary tasks** that need to get done that may not be on our priority list. For example, getting your grading completed may be a priority over doing the dishes. If the dishes get pushed aside every night, they will pile up. Instead, find balance by listing **two to three necessary tasks** so the dishes won't pile up.

My Priorities and Necessary Tasks

Work Life	Social Life	Home Life
Priorities:	Priorities:	Priorities:
Necessary Tasks:	Necessary Tasks:	Necessary Tasks:

Setting Priorities
(leave this page blank to make more copies as needed)

Stress List of Outstanding Tasks

Work Life	Social Life	Home Life

My Priorities and Necessary Tasks

Work Life	Social Life	Home Life
Priorities: Necessary Tasks:	Priorities: Necessary Tasks:	Priorities: Necessary Tasks:

Pause and breathe deeply, then answer one question.
What one thing will I do now?

Creating Balance at Work to Avoid Burnout

Burnout is an increasing international phenomenon. The World Health Organization (WHO) defines burnout as a "syndrome conceptualized as resulting from chronic workplace stress that has not been successfully managed."

According to the WHO, workplace burnout is characterized by:
- Feelings of energy depletion or exhaustion.
- Increased mental distance from one's job or negative feelings towards one's career.
- Reduced professional productivity.

The American Psychological Association (APA) found that two-thirds of people in the workforce report that they experience significant stress while at work, and one out of every four workers has missed work because of stress.

One way to combat burnout is to balance aspects of your workday that you find fulfilling with those you find draining. Once you are more aware of the aspects of work that you find fulfilling and those that drain your emotional energies, you can take action to create balance throughout your workday, and mitigate your risk of burnout. Using the figure below, write down aspects of your work that you find fulfilling and draining.

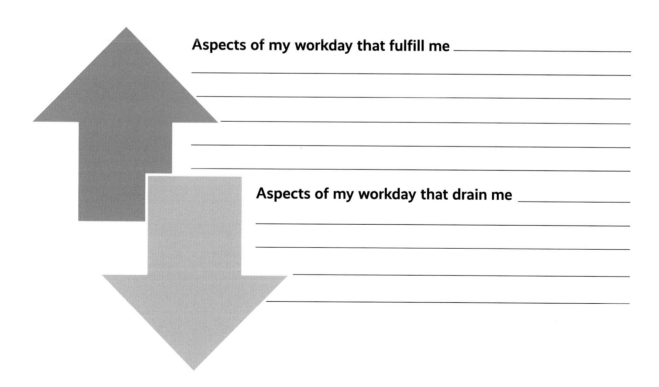

Aspects of my workday that fulfill me _____

_____

_____

_____

_____

Aspects of my workday that drain me _____

_____

_____

_____

_____

You don't have to do anything with the list just yet. For now, it's enough to simply recognize the parts that are fulfilling and those that are draining.

Creating Balance at Work
(leave this page blank to make more copies as needed)

Aspects of my workday that fulfill me

_____

_____

_____

_____

_____

_____

_____

_____

Aspects of my workday that drain me

_____

_____

_____

_____

_____

_____

_____

_____

Advancing Balance at Work to Avoid Burnout

Now, let's do something with your awareness of the fulfilling and draining aspects of your workday.

Think about the aspects that fulfill you and consider how to make them a bigger part of your workday. Pick one fulfilling aspect and write some ideas for how to make it a larger part of your workday.

For example, if you find it satisfying doing activities outside the curriculum or structured time with your students, take the time during recess once or twice a week to play with them instead of doing something that may burden you.

I can make _____ a larger part of my workday by_____

_____

_____

Every job includes unfulfilling tasks that are necessary. Set boundaries to manage the draining aspects of your workday. Look through the tasks you find draining and see if you can delegate them to others or cross them off your list entirely. For example, if creating seasonal bulletin boards causes you to stress, see if you can find some art students to help you.

Draining tasks **I have to do**	Draining tasks **I can delegate**	Draining tasks **I can say no to**

As long as the fulfilling aspects of your day outweigh the draining aspects, you will be buffered against burnout.

Advancing Balance

(leave this page blank to make more copies as needed)

Draining tasks **I have to do**	Draining tasks **I can delegate**	Draining tasks **I can say no to**

Breathe deeply and
notice your inner and outer self.
Commit to being
fully present in this moment.

A Healthy Work-Life Balance

According to Mental Health America, more than one in four Americans describe themselves as "super stressed" while trying to balance work, personal life, and family responsibilities. Most people say their lives would be improved if they had a healthy work-life balance, but what is work-life balance and, more importantly, how does one achieve it?

Finding balance between work and life responsibilities involves alleviating potential stressors in the workplace and at home and by practicing self-care throughout the day.

It's important to be productive at work and minimize the need to "take work home." There is only so much that one person can do, and stressing about unfinished tasks will only diminish your overall productivity. Give yourself some grace. Set clear goals for yourself and when needed, go back to the previous two Graphic Organizers to adjust your priorities. At the very least, include brain and movement breaks throughout your day and lighten your mood by playing relaxing music to help sustain you throughout the day.

Starting today, I can reduce stress at work by...

1. _____
2. _____
3. _____

Moving towards work-life balance also means reducing stress at home and in your social life. Strategic use of time should also apply to how you prioritize things at home. Are you taking responsibility for all the chores at home? Do you need to call a family meeting to ask for help? Let them know that their support is integral for your wellbeing.

Starting today, I can reduce stress at home by...

1. _____
2. _____
3. _____

Remember that self-care also includes how you meet your needs for strong social bonds with friends and family members. Are you spending your social time with people who fill your cup, or are your social relationships and activities another source of stress?

Starting today, I can reduce stress in my social life by...

1. _____
2. _____
3. _____

When needed, seek professional help for mental health issues that may be standing in the way of achieving your wellness goals.

Reducing Stress
(leave this page blank to make more copies as needed)

Starting today, I can reduce stress at WORK by...

1. _____
   _____
   _____

2. _____
   _____
   _____

3. _____
   _____
   _____

Starting today, I can reduce stress at HOME by...

1. _____
   _____
   _____

2. _____
   _____
   _____

3. _____
   _____
   _____

Starting today, I can reduce stress in my SOCIAL LIFE by...

1. _____
   _____
   _____

2. _____
   _____
   _____

3. _____
   _____
   _____

While you may not be in control of what is happening around you, you are in control of how you respond.

Creating Communities of Care

What is a Community of Care?

While a community of care may sound self-explanatory, it's essential to understand the definition to see how transformative having your own community of care can be in bringing wellness to your life. A community of care goes beyond just having someone to talk with. It also includes having a group of people who can provide you with practical assistance like meals, home repairs, or childcare. It also means a group of people checking in on your mental health and helping you find assistance when you need it.

There will be times when you won't be able to do it alone. At some point, the load at work or home is going to be too much to bear and will threaten your wellbeing. This is when your community of care steps in to help restore balance. Having a community of care in place before you need them is a proactive strategy to ensure that searching for assistance is not an additional stressor in your times of greatest need.

How Do I Create my Community of Care?

You can begin creating your community of care with one or two "self-care buddies." These should be friends or family members that you talk to and spend time with regularly. Invite one or both of them over to do a self-care activity together, such as exercising or cooking. Invite them to check in with you about your self-care journey and do the same for them.

As time progresses, add more people from different areas of your life. Collaborate with a co-worker to ease each other's stress at work. Trade child-care with a friend or neighbor so each of you can get one Saturday afternoon off each month. When ready, begin thinking about new relationships you may want to cultivate; maybe there is someone who is in the same class at the gym or a mom you always see at drop-off. These are people who may share the same interests and values as you and could potentially become part of your community of care.

My Community of Care

My needs from my community: *As you think about who to include in your community, first decide which areas you need help with the most. For example, childcare, transportation, or an exercise buddy.*

My buddy community: *Who are your closest friends and family that could join you in the self-care process right away? What is one collective self-care activity that all would enjoy?*

My wider community: *Think about people who have offered you support in different areas of your life, such as work, in your neighborhood, or an organization where you volunteer. Who do you want to put more effort into developing a relationship with to make them part of your community of care?*

My future community: *Consider the people that you see regularly because of shared interests and schedules. Pick one person that you want to begin developing a relationship with and reach out to connect.*

My Community of Care
(leave this page blank to make more copies as needed)

My needs from my community: As you think about who to include in your community, first decide which areas you need help with the most. For example, childcare, transportation, or an exercise buddy.

My buddy community: Who are your closest friends and family that could join you in the self-care process right away? What is one collective self-care activity that all would enjoy?

My wider community: Think about people who have offered you support in different areas of your life, such as work, in your neighborhood, or an organization where you volunteer. Who do you want to put more effort into developing a relationship with to make them part of your community of care?

My future community: Consider the people that you see regularly because of shared interests and schedules. Pick one person that you want to begin developing a relationship with and reach out to connect.

Breathe deeply and *live* *in the present moment.*

Making Conscious Social Choices

As important as it is to be surrounded by positive and supportive people, it's equally crucial to avoid toxic people. Toxic relationships can seriously threaten your physical and mental health. That said, sometimes it's not easy leaving a toxic relationship. Consider these tips for recognizing and ending toxic relationships.

Start with Self-Love

First, you must reflect on your relationship with yourself before thinking about your relationships with others. This will enable you to make decisions about your relationships based on your belief in your own self-worth. Do you give yourself the same grace that you give others? Do you believe that you are deserving of safe, supportive, and healthy relationships?

Write yourself an affirmation that defines the quality of the relationships you deserve to guide you through the process of analyzing your current relationships:

I deserve relationships that _____

_____

_____

_____

Recognize Toxic Relationships

Relationships are an integral part of every aspect of our daily lives, from family to friends to co-workers. Here are some red flags to be on the lookout for when trying to recognize a toxic relationship:

- How do you feel when you are with this individual? Do you feel supported and valued, or put down and ignored?
- How does this person respond to feedback? Do they take into account your needs when you express them, or do they dismiss them? Do they regularly become angry or agitated?
- How does this individual deal with conflict? Do they take responsibility for their mistakes, or do they blame you or others? Can this individual move on from conflict, or do they hold grudges and act spitefully?
- How does this individual treat others? Are they courteous to strangers or rude and dismissive? Do they talk positively about others when they are not around or put them down?

Important Note: If the behaviors of anyone in your life make you feel unsafe or are affecting your wellbeing to the point where your ability to live your life in the way you want is affected, you may be in an abusive relationship. If you think you may be in an abusive relationship, please reach out for help. One way you can get help is by calling the National Domestic Violence Hotline at 1-800-799-7233 or TTY 1-800-787-322.

Fill Your Circle with Positivity

Crowd out toxic relationships by seeking out positive ones. In the table below, fill in the boxes with as many different names as possible. Repeat names of people who fill multiple roles. It's OK if you don't currently have strong relationships with these people. The first step is noticing the positive people around you.

Someone who smiles at me when I see them	*Someone who supports my goals*	*Someone who has the same hobbies as me*	*Someone who listens to me*
Someone who makes me laugh	*Someone I can cry around*	*Someone who gives good compliments*	*Someone who offers me help*
Someone I admire	*Someone who has asked for my feedback*	*Someone who enjoys helping others*	*Someone who has the same goals as me*

Now, using the list of names above, sort them based on relationship status:

*People with whom I **already have close relationships:***	*People with whom I **want to build a closer relationship:***

My Circle of Positive People

(leave this page blank to make more copies as needed)

Notice the positive people around you:

Someone who smiles at me when I see them	Someone who supports my goals	Someone who has the same hobbies as me	Someone who listens to me
Someone who makes me laugh	Someone I can cry around	Someone who gives good compliments	Someone who offers me help
Someone I admire	Someone who has asked for my feedback	Someone who enjoys helping others	Someone who has the same goals as me

Using the list of names above, sort them based on relationship status:

People with whom I **already have close relationships:**	People with whom I **want to build a closer relationship:**

You always have your breath.
Breathe out worry.
Breathe in peace.

Setting Healthy Relationship Boundaries at Work

Oftentimes we have limited control over who we have as co-workers, and because we spend so many hours at work, toxic co-worker relationships can seriously harm our wellbeing. While you may not be able to avoid toxic people at work, you can set limits on the type of relationship that you have with them.

Take a moment to reflect on the co-workers that you engage with regularly. As you think about each, make a note of the ones who trigger an emotional or physiological stress response.

Write down the three people who evoke the strongest negative reaction in you or whose actions are the most bothersome to you. Make notes of what you can do to set boundaries and relieve some of the interpersonal stress.

Name of person	Identify what they do that causes you distress	What are at least two boundaries that you could put in place to minimize the distress?	What would be the best way to communicate your boundaries to them?

Healthy Relationship Boundaries at Work
(leave this page blank to make more copies as needed)

Name of person	Identify what they do that causes you distress	What are at least two boundaries that you could put in place to minimize the distress?	What would be the best way to communicate your boundaries to them?

Breathe...
Be in the present
moment *and live*
neither in your
past regrets nor
uncertain future.

Start a Morning Journal Practice

Journaling can take on many different forms and serve many purposes, each of which can help improve your wellbeing. For instance, bullet journals can help you track your self-care goals and organize your schedule; gratitude journals can make you become acutely aware of what really matters in your life; and an affirmation journal can remind you to make yourself a priority and practice self-compassion. Here are some ways that journaling in the morning can help start your day with self-care. Choose the ideas most relevant for you.

Journaling Ideas

Brain Dump Journal. When you feel overwhelmed, start your workday with a brain dump to have a more productive and less stressed day. Brain dumps allow you to capture all of your thoughts on the page, so you don't need to consume mental energy keeping them in your head. Once you have written them down, it will be easier to prioritize your tasks and goals for the day.

Bullet Journal. Bullet journals are basically organized lists that let you track your progress towards a goal. This goal could be to increase your productivity, improve your health, or complete a long-term project. By having prioritized lists, you can focus on finishing the most important tasks, rather than spending time trying to decide how to spend your time.

Positive Affirmation Journal. Positive affirmation journals are a way of tapping into positive emotions about yourself, your abilities, and your life circumstances. When writing positive affirmations, it's vital to keep them short and repeat them often. Simple prompts can lead to the most powerful affirmations:

1. I am _____

2. I will _____

3. I can _____

Gratitude Journal. Gratitude journals can help you to be mindful of what you are thankful for in your life. When doing gratitude journaling, stay fully engaged in what you are writing about rather than just going through the motions. It's most effective to go deep on one subject instead of just writing a long list. Here are five prompts to get you started:

1. Write about a person for whom you are grateful.
2. Write about your skills and abilities that make you proud of yourself.
3. Write about something you learned this week for which you are grateful.
4. Write about a time you laughed uncontrollably.
5. Write about the positive changes that have occurred in your life over the past year, and be grateful for them.

My Morning Self-Care Journal

Brain dump to begin the day

Self-care activities for the day

Top three priorities for today

Things I cannot control

Things I can control

One action I can take today on the things over which I have some control

Daily positive affirmation (I am..., I can..., I will...)

One thing I am grateful for today

My Morning Self-Care Journal
(leave this page blank to make more copies as needed)

Brain dump to begin the day

Self-care activities for the day	Top three priorities for today

Things I cannot control	Things I can control

One action I can take today on the things over which I have some control

Daily positive affirmation (I am..., I can..., I will...)

One thing I am grateful for today

Choose to relax and *let go.*

Mitigating Workplace Burnout, Part 1

Workplace burnout is becoming more common in our increasingly competitive globalized society. Symptoms of burnout often build slowly so they may be hard to recognize, and if not addressed, your body and brain will eventually shut down and prevent you from continuing to harm yourself. For those in caring professions like education, it's even more likely that you will experience burnout due to the empathetic nature of people that go into those careers.

Risk Factor No. 1: You are passionate about your career. Many of us find fulfillment in our work; however, when we start "living to work" that passion can become a risk factor for burnout. When you are hyper-focused on work or obsessed even, basic needs like eating lunch or sleeping at least seven to eight hours may get pushed aside.

To create a healthier balance, use the skills that make you successful at work to plan for self-care. Set self-care goals and plan the same way you would a work task. It can be as simple as setting a timer or calendar alert to remind you to eat lunch or do a daily meditation. Go back to *Scheduling Self-Care* and plan your monthly, weekly, and daily self-care practices.

Risk Factor No. 2: You compare yourself to your colleagues. People who are highly motivated or ambitious at work are also likely to want to keep up with their co-workers. When you begin to compare yourself to your colleagues, you diminish your own feelings of success. Additionally, as everyone in a competitive workplace works harder to compete, the workload increases for everyone without any increases in workplace satisfaction—thus leading to burnout.

Begin to eliminate unhealthy workplace competition by defining your strengths and the unique ways you contribute to the team without competing with other people's talents. Then, focus on how your students, school, and team benefit from your contributions.

What are my strengths and the unique ways that I contribute to my school/team?

How do my strengths benefit/improve my school/team?

Find ways to collaborate with your colleagues, which will increase productivity and create a sense of team unity rather than competitiveness.

Breathe deeply and give
yourself time to

calm your mind.

The only thing you
have to do is

take one next step.

Mitigating Workplace Burnout, Part 2

Let's continue working through two more risk factors and supportive solutions.

Risk Factor No 3: You don't fit the mold. Many workplaces, especially competitive or "high stakes" workplaces, tend to have an ideal type or "model employee." These models can be created by workplace culture, specific policies, or a boss who prefers a particular working style. You may experience burnout if you find yourself trying too hard to fit in, especially if you have a different personality type or working style than the "model employee."

You can cope with not "fitting in" by using self-affirmations and reminding yourself to keep a growth mindset. Use self-affirmations regularly to remind yourself that you are there for a reason, that you were hired for your unique strengths, and you are valuable in the workplace.

Write affirmations and remind yourself of them when you doubt yourself at work:

For example: I was hired for all of the talents I have to contribute to my team.

_____

_____

_____

_____

_____

Next, fill in the blanks below to practice a "growth mindset." A growth mindset is the belief that, while you currently may lack a specific skill, you can grow to meet those expectations with focused work. A growth mindset sounds like:

While I cannot yet _____

_____

I am going to work hard at _____

_____

so that I will be able to _____

_____

Risk Factor No. 4: You don't set workplace boundaries. When you work in an organization that values hard work and going the extra mile, it can be hard to set boundaries for what you are willing and able to do. Setting boundaries can be particularly challenging in workplaces with too much work to do and not enough staff to get it done. Remember that you will be more productive, and thus of more value to your workplace, if you prioritize taking care of yourself.

Begin establishing boundaries at work by defining those boundaries for yourself. Decide:

What is an acceptable number of hours for me to work each week? _____

_____

What is an acceptable work schedule for me? _____

_____   _____

What life experiences outside of work do I need to prioritize? _____

_____

What work tasks leave me feeling fulfilled? Which ones do I need to say no to? _____

_____

_____

Once you are clear on your boundaries, make a plan to hold yourself accountable, and use assertive-communication techniques, detailed in the next Self-Care Graphic Organizer, to express your needs to your supervisor and/or co-workers.

Pause and breathe deeply
Notice what you hear, smell,
touch, and see. Appreciate this
present moment.

Assertive Communication

An essential part of self-care is effectively communicating your needs and boundaries. Assertive communication is a style of communication in which you clearly and confidently advocate for your needs while still considering others' needs. This differs from aggressive communication in which someone dismisses the needs of others, and differs from passive-aggressive communication in which the needs of the communicator are unclear.

Traits of Assertive Communicators

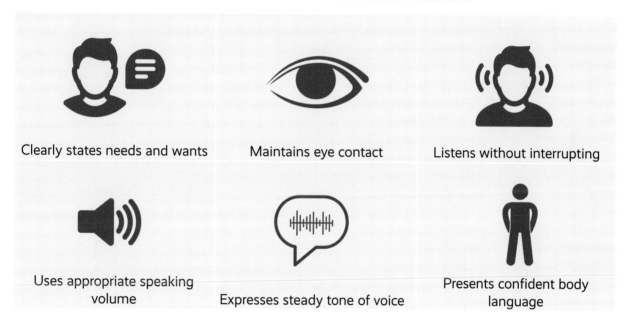

Clearly states needs and wants

Maintains eye contact

Listens without interrupting

Uses appropriate speaking volume

Expresses steady tone of voice

Presents confident body language

Practicing "I statements" is an effective way to communicate assertively:

1. Start by taking responsibility for your own emotions and needs: *"I feel..." or "I need..."*
2. State the behavior or situation that is causing a negative reaction: *"When you..."*
3. State what it is that you find challenging about the behavior or situation: *"Because..."*
4. Offer an alternative or compromise that meets your needs: *"It would really help me if..."*

Using the formula above, you can change a passive statement into an assertive statement. For example:

Instead of saying: *"You never listen to my ideas!"*
Try saying: *"I feel like I am not being heard in our discussions when you start talking before I am finished because I have more to say that might be beneficial to us. I would really like it if you listened while I am talking, and I will do the same for you."*

Assertive Communication Practice

Describe your communication style. Are you typically more direct in ways that some people may experience as aggressive, or do you find it challenging to express your needs? Are you good at listening to others, or do you feel the need to dominate the conversation to get your point across?

Think about a recent situation where you had a hard time expressing your needs.

*What made communication challenging in that situation?*_____

_____

_____

_____

Which traits of assertive communicators could you have used in that situation to help you express your needs and boundaries more confidently? _____

_____

_____

_____

What are some "I statements" that you could have used to express your needs? _____

_____

_____

_____

The next time you need to express your needs and communicate your personal or professional boundaries, try writing a few "I statements" before talking with that person.

Assertive Communication Plan

(leave this page blank to make more copies as needed)

Think about a recent situation where you are having a hard time expressing your needs.

What is making communication challenging in this situation?
Which traits of assertive communicators can you use in this situation to help you express your needs and boundaries more confidently?
What are some "I statements" that you can use to express your needs?

Slow down and appreciate this one present moment.

Turning Obstacles into Opportunities

Challenging experiences can be obstacles that hinder you or become opportunities that push you to grow. Challenges are obstacles when they are barriers to your professional, personal, or overall life advancement. The stress they create can harm your physical, mental, emotional, and spiritual wellness.

Here is a suggestion to help you turn some of your biggest obstacles into opportunities:

Break it down. A challenge is more likely to become an obstacle when you see it as one large problem. To buffer against becoming overwhelmed by crisis moments, step back and look at the ways the crisis has affected you. As you write them down, your brain will begin to generate potential solutions right away. This can help you identify the steps that you'll need to take to overcome the challenge.

Initially, you may only see how it hinders you. Turning obstacles into opportunities requires that you begin to see them as a chance to learn and grow. What if in the end your challenge enables you to improve some aspect of yourself or show that you are stronger, braver, and smarter than you realize?

What is one obstacle that is preventing you from a personal or professional goal?

List the reasons or factors why this obstacle is holding you back:	Imagine one thing that you can do/learn/ask for that could help to resolve this issue:

Ask yourself: What can I learn from this challenge?

Take decisive action. After taking time to break it down and imagine possible solutions, roll up your sleeves and get to work, making sure that this is not a missed opportunity to strengthen your existing skills or learn new ones.

Turn Obstacles Into Opportunities

(leave this page blank to make more copies as needed)

What is one obstacle that is preventing you from a personal or professional goal?	
List the reasons or factors why this obstacle is holding you back:	Imagine one thing that you can do/learn/ask for that could help to resolve this issue:
Ask yourself: What can I learn from this challenge?	

Take decisive action. After taking time to break it down and imagine possible solutions, roll up your sleeves and get to work, making sure that this is not a missed opportunity to strengthen your existing skills or learn new ones.

The present is the most important moment.

Breathe deeply and bring yourself into the present.

Start an Evening Journal Practice

As discussed, journaling can improve your self-care. Consider adding a few minutes of journaling to your evening routine. Choose the ideas most relevant for you.

Brain Dump Journal. Practice the strategy of ending your day with a brain dump to allow yourself to "turn off" and have a more restful night. Brain dumps allow you to capture all of your thoughts on the page so you don't need to spend effort holding them in your head. Once you have gotten out all of your thoughts, it will be easier to let go of those thoughts that may be unsettling or don't need your immediate attention.

Bullet Journal. Bullet journals are basically organized lists that let you track your progress towards a goal. This goal could be to increase your productivity, improve your health, or complete a long-term project. By having prioritized lists, you can focus on finishing the most important tasks rather than spending time trying to decide how to spend your time.

Positive Affirmation Journal. Positive affirmation journals are a way of tapping into positive emotions about yourself, your abilities, and your life circumstances. Writing a few affirmations may be particularly helpful at the end of a hard day. When writing positive affirmations, it is vital to keep them short and repeat them often. Simple prompts can lead to the most powerful affirmations:

- I am _____
  _____

- I will _____
  _____

- I can _____
  _____

Gratitude Journal. Gratitude journals can help you to be mindful of what you are thankful for in your life. When doing gratitude journaling, stay fully engaged in what you are writing about rather than just going through the motions. It's most effective to go deep on one subject instead of just writing a long list. Here are five prompts to get you started:

1. Write about a person for whom you are grateful.
2. Write about your skills and abilities that make you proud of yourself.
3. Write about something you learned this week for which you are grateful.
4. Write about a time you laughed uncontrollably.
5. Write about the positive changes that have occurred in your life over the past year, and be grateful for them.

My Evening Self-Care Journal

Brain dump to end the day

Self-care activities for tomorrow

Top three priorities for tomorrow

Things I can't control

Things I can control

One action I can take tomorrow on the things over which I have some control

Daily positive affirmation (I can..., I will..., I am...)

One thing I am grateful for today

My Evening Self-Care Journal

(leave this page blank to make more copies as needed)

Brain dump to end the day

Self-care activities for tomorrow	Top three priorities for tomorrow

Things I can't control	Things I can control

One action I can take tomorrow on the things over which I have some control

Daily positive affirmation (I can..., I will..., I am...)

One thing I am grateful for today

Breathe out discouragement.
Breathe in *hope*.

Mindful Walking Practices

Getting out to take a walk is a great form of self-care. Research shows that being out in nature sends calming signals to your brain. Practicing mindfulness while walking can boost nature's benefits for relieving stress and recharging your mind and body.

There are many ways to be mindful while walking. The first step is slowing down to intentionally notice your surroundings. As you walk, become aware of what your senses are taking in—sight, touch, smell, hearing, and taste. Bring yourself fully into the present moment.

Notice...
- The tiny details around you such as a bird up in a high branch.
- How the sun or breeze feels on your skin.
- How your feet feel as they make contact with the ground.
- The smell of fresh rain or a coffeeshop nearby.
- The sound of children playing, a car going past, or leaves rustling under your feet.
- The taste of salt in the air near the ocean.

As you begin to become more mindful on your walk, notice how your mind and body feel. Have your thoughts become more quiet or focused? Do your muscles feel more relaxed? Has your breathing become deeper? These are all signs that your body is feeling more relaxed.

Consider documenting your walk by sketching images to remind you of what you noticed, writing notes or a poem about how you felt, or about the thoughts that came to mind.

Document Your Walk

Use this space to document a walk. Be intentional and let yourself know in advance that you will document the walk before you head out. Draw images, write notes or a poem.

What did you notice?
How did you feel before, during, after the walk?
What thoughts came to your mind during the walk?

Document Your Walk

(leave this page blank to make more copies as needed)

Use this space to document a walk. Be intentional and let yourself know in advance that you will document the walk before you head out. Draw images, write notes or a poem.

What did you notice?
How did you feel before, during, after the walk?
What thoughts came to your mind during the walk?

How are you doing in this moment?

Don't answer just yet.

Breathe.

Breathe.

Breathe.

Now, be honest with yourself.

Time is Not an Obstacle

Now that you are about halfway through the Self-Care Graphic Organizers, let's revisit the amount of time you set aside for self-care.

The times you feel the busiest and most over-extended are when you need self-care the most. It's important to make time for self-care, even when you think you don't have time, to buffer against burnout. Self-care is about slowing down, listening to your mind and body, and attending to your needs. There are many ways to integrate self-care into your day, in ten minutes, thirty minutes, an hour, or a full afternoon. As you try some of these practices, work on including some of them into your routine to ensure that you meet your needs no matter how busy you are. Here are some ideas:

Ten Minutes of Self-Care

All you need is ten minutes to feel the positive benefits of self-care. If you have a hard time fitting in self-care, try waking up ten minutes earlier or using part of your lunch break for self-care. Some activities you can complete in ten minutes include:

- Meditating
- Doing yoga or stretches
- Mindfully sipping hot tea or ice water

- Practicing deep breathing
- Journaling
- Sitting outside or in sunny window

Thirty Minutes of Self-Care

Finding just thirty minutes in your schedule to spend on yourself will help you feel focused and productive throughout your day. Some activities you can complete in thirty minutes are:

- Taking a long shower or bath
- Cooking your favorite meal
- Exercising at home

- Applying a sheet mask and turning on your favorite TV show or podcast
- Reading a book

An Hour of Self-Care

Claiming an hour for self-care, even if just once a week, can produce benefits for your overall wellbeing. Some activities you can complete in sixty minutes are:

- Trying a new recipe
- Taking a fitness class
- Working on a hobby

- Meeting a friend for lunch
- Organizing your workspace
- Sitting peacefully on a park bench

An Afternoon of Self-Care

Try to claim three to four hours to yourself once a month. This extended amount of time allows you to disconnect from stressors and reflect on what you need to do to reach your wellbeing goals. You will be able to recharge and come back to your responsibilities with new energy. Here are some ideas for an afternoon of self-care:

- Go on a hike or explore a new neighborhood in your city
- Spend an afternoon at the spa

- Clean out a cluttered spot in your home and donate what you no longer need
- Take an art, music, or some other class

Time for Self-Care

Try to list two self-care activities that would be beneficial for you in each of the time blocks:

10 minutes for self-care	• _____
	• _____
30 minutes for self-care	• _____
	• _____
An hour for self-care	• _____
	• _____
An afternoon for self-care	• _____
	• _____

Time for Self-Care
(leave this page blank to make more copies as needed)

List two self-care activities that would be beneficial for you in each time block:

10 minutes for self-care	_____ _____ _____ _____ _____
30 minutes for self-care	_____ _____ _____ _____ _____
An hour for self-care	_____ _____ _____ _____ _____
An afternoon for self-care	_____ _____ _____ _____ _____

Bring your awareness to the

present

moment.

Understanding and Recognizing Compassion Fatigue

Compassion fatigue reduces your ability to connect with others and be empathetic in response to their needs for care. It can be caused by repeated exposure to the stories of other's traumatic experiences and the demands of meeting their needs. Sadly, too many students carry with them the stress of hunger, abuse, violence, neglect, illness, death of loved ones, and more. The daily emotional toll of concern for these students, the reminders of the obstacles they face, and the distress of genuine limitations in your ability to meet their needs can cause compassion fatigue.

Knowing and recognizing the signs of compassion fatigue in yourself and your colleagues is the first step to mitigating and managing the cost of being in a helping profession. Review the signs of compassion fatigue listed below and reflect on whether you are experiencing any of them. This can help you prioritize yourself while caring for others.

Signs of Compassion Fatigue	Is this a regular experience?	
Emotional Signs		
Feeling overwhelmed by hopelessness and powerlessness about others	Yes	No
Feeling overwhelmed by irritability and anxiety about others' needs		
Feeling emotionally or physically exhausted, burnt out, or numb		
Having limited tolerance for stress		
Cognitive Signs		
Constant thinking or dwelling on the suffering of others		
Constant self-blame or thoughts of "I should or could have done more"		
Changes in beliefs about self, others, the world, or the meaning in life		
Difficulty focusing, thinking, or making decisions		
Behavioral Signs		
Self-isolation and withdrawal		
Coping by self-medicating with non-prescribed substance use		
Escalating relationship conflicts		
Reduced pleasure in previously enjoyed activities and work satisfaction		
Physical Signs		
Chronic physical and emotional exhaustion		
Being tense, agitated, and on edge		
Weight loss or weight gain		
Frequent illness and lowered immune system health		

Periodically Assess Your Level of Compassion Fatigue

(leave this page blank to make more copies as needed)

Signs of Compassion Fatigue	Is this a regular experience?	
Emotional Signs		
Feeling overwhelmed by hopelessness and powerlessness about others	Yes	No
Feeling overwhelmed by irritability and anxiety about others' needs		
Feeling emotionally or physically exhausted, burnt out, or numb		
Having limited tolerance for stress		
Cognitive Signs		
Constant thinking or dwelling on the suffering of others		
Constant self-blame or thoughts of "I should or could have done more"		
Changes in beliefs about self, others, the world, or the meaning in life		
Difficulty focusing, thinking, or making decisions		
Behavioral Signs		
Self-isolation and withdrawal		
Coping by self-medicating with non-prescribed substance use		
Escalating relationship conflicts		
Reduced pleasure in previously enjoyed activities and work satisfaction		
Physical Signs		
Chronic physical and emotional exhaustion		
Being tense, agitated, and on edge		
Weight loss or weight gain		
Frequent illness and lowered immune system health		

Instead of forcing yourself to
"let it go"
breathe deeply and
"let it be".

Mitigating Compassion Fatigue

Compassion fatigue creeps up slowly. We often don't recognize that we are nearing our emotional

capacity of extending care to others until we begin to act out in unhelpful ways. You probably don't realize the many ways that you are extending yourself to care for others, such as being there as a listening ear for friends, tending to the needs of family members, or volunteering to support an event or organization.

One way of mitigating compassion fatigue is by establishing a practice of regular self-check-ins. Use the Self-Care Graphic Organizer on the next page to regularly check in with yourself so that compassion fatigue doesn't build up.

Consider adding this self-check-in to your weekly calendar, for example, on Fridays, to see where you are at the end of your workweek. You can also add it to your Monday calendar to see where you are at the start of your workweek.

Compassion fatigue develops over time, and the same goes for recovery. Sometimes taking a vacation or a personal day can be restoring, but more often, a gradual shift to a stress-reduction lifestyle is necessary.

Stress Build-Up Check-In

Take a three-breath pause before completing these questions.

Make time to regularly revisit, reassess, revise, and adjust the stressors in your life.

On a scale of 1 to 10, where is my stress level at?
1 = I feel totally relaxed and on top of everything
10 = I'm on edge and near my breaking point all the time.

I am at a _____ because...

What are the top three stressors in my life?

Do I have control over any of them?

What stress resiliency strategies, such as meditation, yoga, or breathing exercises can I use?

What stress-reduction actions, such as cutting back on or stopping things that are stressful can I implement?

Stress Build-Up Check-In

(leave this page blank to make more copies as needed)

Take a three-breath pause before completing these questions.

On a scale of 1 to 10, where is my stress level at? **1** = I feel totally relaxed and on top of everything **10** = I'm on edge and near my breaking point all the time. I am at a _____ because...	What are the top three stressors in my life? Do I have control over any of them?

What stress resiliency strategies, such as meditation, yoga, or breathing exercises can I use?

What stress-reduction actions, such as cutting back on or stopping things that are stressful can I implement?

Mindfulness is paying attention, on purpose, in the present moment. Without judgment pay attention to your thoughts and feelings in the present moment.

Self-Compassion

We grant ourselves self-compassion by reining in the voice of the inner critic. Educators demand a lot of themselves in the face of ever-increasing pressures, time-sensitive demands, and dwindling resources. Learning to extend compassion to yourself can be a powerful personal change that can foster resilience and wellbeing. People who practice self-compassion experience fewer negative emotions and are more likely to stay emotionally balanced under stressful situations.

Kristin Neff, co-author of *The Mindful Self-Compassion Workbook*, lists three components to self-compassion. The first component is **self-kindness**, treating yourself with the same care and concern you would extend to a loved one. If negative self-talk has become commonplace, you need to be intentional and deliberate to replace it with compassionate self-talk. Pay attention to the ways you may slip into berating yourself. Imagine a close friend retelling you the events of their challenging day and think of how you might respond to them.

The second component is **recognizing our common humanity**. Often when something wrong or stressful happens, we tell ourselves, "This should not be happening." The reality is that education is an incredibly challenging profession, and we will often get it wrong. The most compassionate response you can give yourself is to remember that educating children and adolescents requires a lot of skill, and that you are doing the best you can despite the obstacles. Also, acknowledge the ways that you are constantly learning how to do it better.

The third component is **mindfulness**. Simply put, mindfulness is awareness of yourself in the present moment. With regular practice, mindfulness can act as a buffer between the challenges and stressors that educators face and the negative thoughts and feelings that naturally arise. Mindfulness can help you become aware of those thoughts and feelings and then choose self-compassion.

Physically remind yourself of your need for self-compassion. Offer the hugs that you give to others to yourself. Wrap your arms around yourself or fold your arms in a non-obvious way that mirrors a hug. Just as you would hug a friend who's having a rough day, this physical gesture of self-compassion is an easy way to soothe and comfort yourself.

Mentally remind yourself of your need for self-compassion. Take an immediate break during a moment of distress by pausing to breathe deeply. Focusing on your breath is one of the best methods of calming yourself during a challenging situation. Very simply, breathe in compassion for yourself and breathe out compassion for others.

Verbally remind yourself of your need for self-compassion. Affirm your humanity and care for yourself out loud when you need to offer self-compassion. Take a moment to read out loud some examples of educator affirmations on the next page.

Educator Affirmations

I am a competent and capable educator. I am confident in my abilities.

I will not worry about the things I cannot control.

It is okay to ask for help. I am not alone.

I am a better person because of my students. My students are better people because of me.

I make a difference in my students' lives.

Everyone is doing the best they can including me.

I am in the right place. I am meant to be an educator. I am meant to be here.

What I do today will make a difference tomorrow.

I make a positive difference in my students' lives.

First and foremost, be kind to myself.

It is OK for the kids to be kids and for me to be myself!

Use your breath to breathe out anxiety and breathe in confidence and strength.

Choices to Improve Your Wellbeing

The Happy Teacher Revolution (happyteacherrevolution.com), a movement that originated in Baltimore, rightfully claims that "teachers should not feel obligated to sacrifice their wholeness or wellbeing in order to perform well professionally." They recommend Vicki Davis' *12 Choices to Help you Step Back from Burnout*. Below is an adapted listing of the 12 choices for you to reflect on regularly to gradually adjust your choices in ways that will improve your wellbeing.

Self-care is the result of active choices. Whenever you feel overwhelmed and distressed about workplace stressors, look over this list to identify opportunities to make choices that will move you toward wellbeing. When you reflect on this list, you can reflect on just one choice or several potential choices. Always try to connect your reflections with actions.

Choices to help you step back from burnout		How did this choice change your stress?	
Choose to be happy	Happiness is a choice. Choose to be the first one to smile at everybody you meet. Choose to greet your students with joy.	Felt a little less stressed	Felt a lot less stressed
Choose to disconnect	Unplug once a week. Be a human being, not a human doing. For example: Leave your phone in the car or put it in a back closet at least one evening each week.	Felt a little less stressed	Felt a lot less stressed
Choose to be mindful	Mindfulness is a powerful and simple stress reducer. Meditate, practice yoga, or pray.	Felt a little less stressed	Felt a lot less stressed
Choose to make time for sleep	Go to sleep early and leave your cell phone somewhere where it won't be tempting to grab it. You can also turn on the "do not disturb" feature.	Felt a little less stressed	Felt a lot less stressed
Choose to get outside and get moving	Exercise is a powerful treatment for depression, diabetes, and anxiety. Even five minutes of being outdoors is shown to boost your mood.	Felt a little less stressed	Felt a lot less stressed

	Choice	How did this choice change your stress?	
Choose to be grateful	Studies show that keeping a gratitude journal will increase your long-term wellbeing more than winning a million dollars.	Felt a little less stressed	Felt a lot less stressed
Choose what to overlook	Understand that you're working with others who are almost, if not more, burned out than you. Therefore, count on everyone being fussy, cranky, and tired. Let it go.	Felt a little less stressed	Felt a lot less stressed
Choose the battles worth fighting	Choose to fight only for what matters. Let go of the pressure you are putting on yourself for something that doesn't really matter.	Felt a little less stressed	Felt a lot less stressed
Choose what to keep doing and what to stop	Remember your mistakes, but keep your eyes facing front toward your current surroundings.	Felt a little less stressed	Felt a lot less stressed
Choose to enjoy relationships that matter	Don't be so busy making a living that you forget to make time for living. Schedule fun time alone, with family members, and with friends.	Felt a little less stressed	Felt a lot less stressed
Choose to make a schedule that matters	Schedule important tasks. The things on your calendar are more likely to be the "done" items.	Felt a little less stressed	Felt a lot less stressed
Choose to finish well	No matter how you started the year, choose to finish it well. This is also your decision.	Felt a little less stressed	Felt a lot less stressed

Unplug and reset. Walk away from whatever you are doing and engage in one minute of mindful deep breathing to reset.

Reduce Your Trauma Inputs

Compassionate self-care is crucial for educators working in schools where substantial numbers of students are actively coping with exposure to adverse and traumatic life experiences. In addition to the regular attention to healthy habits of exercise, sleep, and eating healthy, you will need to intentionally reduce your exposure to learning about the numerous traumatic and tragic events that have come to be too much a part of daily life.

Consider the questions below to assess your level of exposure to secondary trauma that comes from listening to and learning about the stories of others who have directly experienced trauma. Are you exposed to more secondary trauma than your brain and body can handle?
To ensure that you have the psychological and emotional space to hear and respond to your students'

Source of Secondary Trauma	Frequency of Exposure			
	A few times a year	About once a month	About once a week	Daily
Your students telling you about their adverse or traumatic life experiences.				
Colleagues telling you about their students' adverse or traumatic life experiences.				
Spouse in a helping profession telling you about their traumatic stories.				
Traumatic stories on the morning news.				
Traumatic stories on the radio or social media during your commute to work.				
Traumatic stories on the radio or social media during your commute back home.				
Traumatic stories on the evening news.				
Family and friends in a helping profession telling you about their traumatic stories.				
Other sources of stories about people's traumatic experiences.				

stories, make choices to turn off, set boundaries, and limit some of your other sources of secondary trauma inputs.

Take a deep inhale...
Allow one deep exhale...
That is enough...

Leave Unfinished Work at Work

Compassionate self-care includes leaving unfinished work at work, a few evenings a week and a

couple weekends a month. This can be especially difficult when supporting students who are going home to difficult contexts. However, this separation from work is critical because compassion fatigue can arise from constant worry about situations over which you have no control—it wears down your mental and emotional wellbeing.

You will need to actively remind yourself that you cannot and are not expected to meet all your students' needs. You will never have enough time or resources to meet all their needs. Therefore, try your best to end your workday reminding yourself of this because despite doing all that you can, many students' needs will go unmet.

Creating a work-to-home transition routine can help you leave the workday at work so that you can be fully present for your personal needs and the needs of your family, without the weight of self-judgment.

Create a *mindful transition ritual to intentionally pause the stressors of the day* so you can be present for the other aspects of your life that need attention.

If you walk home from work, integrate a transition ritual into your walk home. It can be as simple as intentionally adding a loop around a block by taking a left instead of a right to do some focused deep breathing to clear your mind before opening your front door.

If you drive or take public transportation, make the commute less stressful by adding a podcast or an audiobook, so that the commute adds to instead of detracting from your day. Make sure that whatever you listen to is calming and centering, uplifting and positive, or joyous and funny.

> *Take a moment to make some quick notes about what you can do on your way home from work to pause the stressors of the day.*

Create small moments in your day to be still. Pause and take three deep breaths.

Claim Your Time and Space

Self-care is not about adding one more thing to your to-do list. It's about intentionally reviewing, reorganizing, and revising your to-do list to claim time and space for your wellbeing. You probably have a lot more control over your stressors and your time than you realize.

Complete the table below to brainstorm ways of changing that will improve your wellbeing. Allow yourself a moment to be reflective and creative before writing down your answer to each question. You don't necessarily have to know how you will make it happen, just write down the idea and commit to figuring out how to make it happen.

Things I want to do that would contribute to self-care.	
Things I need to let go of to make space for the things I want to do.	
If I had more time for myself, I would...	
I can claim time for myself by setting limits on...	
Things I want to say "yes" to.	
Things I need to say "no" to.	

Claim Your Time and Space

(leave this page blank to make more copies as needed)

Things I want to do that would contribute to self-care.	
Things I need to let go of to make space for the things I want to do.	
If I had more time for myself, I would...	
I can claim time for myself by setting limits on...	
Things I want to say "yes" to.	
Things I need to say "no" to.	

Pause...
Breathe...
Be...
This moment simply is...

Personal and Professional Strategies for Preventing Burnout

The staff at the We Are Teachers network (weareteachers.com) talked with educators about what they are doing to reduce burnout. They found that many of their strategies focus on preventing their professional lives from becoming their whole lives. Some of their methods were personal. Educators discussed investing in hobbies that have nothing to do with their professional lives to create boundaries and stimulate creativity. Other strategies were professional. Educators discussed ways of reducing the work they need to take home by learning to use assignments that require less grading and being honest with students about when there will be a delay in returning graded assignments.

Complete the table below to see how you can implement a few of the high-value strategies that they listed. More strategies are detailed in their article titled *15 Smart Ways to Prevent Teacher Burnout That Really Work*.

Strategy	How can you put this into practice?
Reflect on whether your use of class time often does not match what you put in your lesson plan. Do you regularly find yourself stressed and anxious about needing more time? If so, search for a few articles on time management for educators and list some of the strategies they share.	

If you are up most nights trying to complete grading, try reducing the number of graded assignments, finding ways to use answer keys to enable students to grade their own assignments in class, and identifying other teaching practices to reduce stress, anxiety, and loss of sleep that results from the pile up of grading.

Set personal development goals. If all your personal activities and hobbies are also about work, it's time to rediscover old or gain new interests that have nothing to do with education.

Electronically disconnect from work. Give yourself permission not to respond to work email when you need a break. It can be from 6 p.m. to 9 p.m., or no emails after 8:30 p.m., or no emails on Sundays. Do what works best for you and your family.

Breathe and
Be right here, right now.

Emotional Check-Ins Throughout Your Day

Educator stress is escalating. A Met Life survey of the American teachers found that in 1985, over

36 percent of teachers reported "being under great stress several days a week or more." When they repeated that same survey in 2012, 51 percent of teachers reported great stress. Who knows what the results will be going forward in the aftermath of the COVID-19 pandemic?

Education is a caring profession, and learning is best accomplished in the context of caring educator-student relationships. The challenge is that the stronger the educator-student relationship, the more at-risk the educator is for being negatively affected by secondary traumatic stress.

You are at increased risk for emotional burnout if: (check off your risk factors)

_____ You have many students who have experienced or are experiencing traumatic events.

_____ You are closely connected to a student(s) who is coping with traumatic events.

_____ A student(s) tells you intense stories of their experience with traumatic events.

_____ You have a heightened level of empathy (sensitivity) to the needs of others.

_____ You are coping with your own trauma and haven't received adequate support.

_____ You tend to neglect or lack awareness of your own emotional needs.

_____ You tend to believe that it's your responsibility to save your students.

Because you are focused on recognizing and responding to your students' emotional needs, it can be difficult to also be aware of how the day's events are impacting your own emotional needs and wellbeing. You must find moments to check-in with yourself to identify, accept, and respond to the range of negative emotions that we all experience throughout the day.

Set external reminders for emotional check-ins throughout your day. Train yourself to pause and reflect on your emotions each time the signal occurs. Signals can include the start of morning announcements, when the last student leaves your class for recess or lunch, or when the last student leaves your class at the end of the day.

Always take one deep breath before you check-in with yourself, and whenever possible, take three deep breaths.

Complete the emotional check-in prompts on the next page to become more self-aware of your emotional wellbeing throughout the day.

Emotional Check-In Prompts

External cues that will serve as my emotional check-in reminders.	
Physical sensations that I will scan my body for to identify my level of stress and distress.	
Questions that I will as myself to identify my level of stress and distress.	
Emotion words that I will reflect on to identify my level of stress and distress.	Upset, calm, angry, happy, worn-out, pleased, anxious, motivated, discouraged, etc.?

When you feel unsettled, but can't identify the feeling, try using the wheel of emotions on the next page to reflect on your emotional responses to what may be happening during your day.

Color-Coded Wheel of Emotions

Increase your emotional self-awareness by first locating the primary emotion in the center of the wheel closest to how you are feeling in the moment. Then, follow that color band out to the edge to identify the corresponding more complex emotions that you may be feeling.

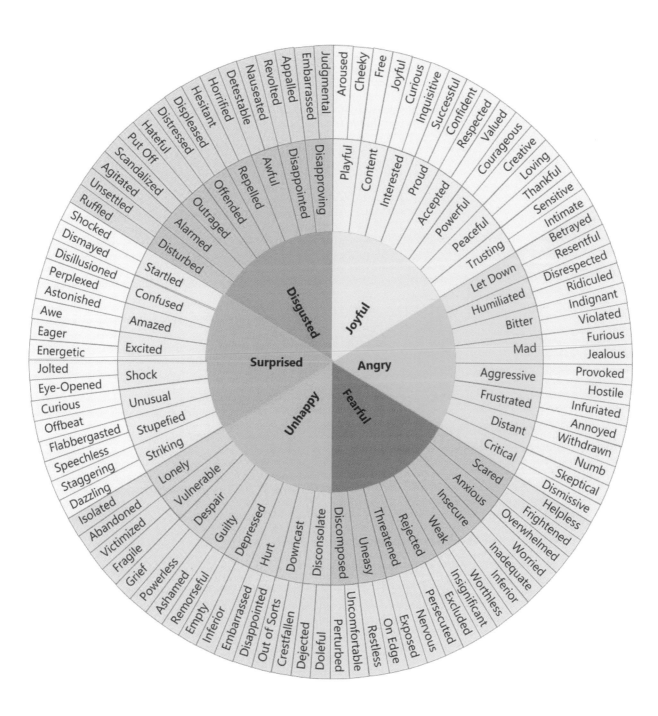

Notice the stillness *at the peak of your inhale...* *Notice the calm* *at the end of your exhale...*

Self-Care with Maslow's Hierarchy of Needs

Most educators are familiar with Maslow's Hierarchy of Needs, which identifies lower-level needs

that first need to be filled for a person to be supported and motivated to grow and fulfill higher-level needs. The figure below lists a couple examples of self-care practices that can help you meet each need. As you read through, think of one practice that you currently aren't doing but want to start doing, for each level of need.

SELF-ACTUALIZATION NEEDS like creativity that can be expressed intellectually, physically, or emotionally. Practices: Join a club or take a class that has no connection to your work; claim time for activities that bring you joy.

ESTEEM NEEDS like dignity, achievement, and independence. Practices: Surround yourself with co-workers who validate one another; be intentional about recognizing the big and little things that you do for others.

BELONGING NEEDS like friendship, intimacy, trust, and acceptance. Practices: Schedule a weekly call date with family and friends; start an exercise-buddies crew with colleagues.

SAFETY NEEDS like order, protection, and medical care. Practices: Create a safety plan for a student with behavioral challenges; create a family appointments calendar.

PHYSIOLOGICAL NEEDS like food, water, shelter, and clothing. Practices: Always carry a water bottle; go to bed early enough to wake up feeling fully rested.

Now think of some practices that you want to begin doing and use the table on the next page to make a sustainable plan for how you will bring each practice into fruition. Start from the bottom up and focus first on practices that meet your physiological and safety needs so that you will have the energy to attend to your higher-level needs.

Self-Care Practices Matched to Maslow's Hierarchy of Needs

Try adding reminders and alerts in your calendar to help you follow through on your plans.

Plan for one **self-actualization** practice that can enhance my wellbeing:

Plan for one **safety** practice that can enhance my wellbeing:

Plan for one **belonging** practice that can enhance my wellbeing:

Plan for one **safety** practice that can enhance my wellbeing:

Plan for one **physiological** practice that can enhance my wellbeing:

Self-Care Practices Matched to Maslow's Hierarchy of Needs
(leave this page blank to make more copies as needed)

Try adding reminders and alerts in your calendar to help you follow through on your plans.

Plan for one **self-actualization** practice that can enhance my wellbeing:

Plan for one **safety** practice that can enhance my wellbeing:

Plan for one **belonging** practice that can enhance my wellbeing:

Plan for one **safety** practice that can enhance my wellbeing:

Plan for one **physiological** practice that can enhance my wellbeing:

Through your deep calming breaths, stress loses power.

Cognitive Reframing to Reduce Stress

Cognitive reframing is the active use of strategies to change how we think about and experience life situations. It can be an effective strategy for lightening the emotional load associated with life's many stressors, especially when the stressor is unavoidable.

For example, a long drive home from work can aggravate your frustrations or it can provide you the time needed to release the day's frustrations, depending on how you look at it. When you think about the drive home as an opportunity to de-stress and then listen to a mindfulness podcast during the drive you have *not only actively reframed but also changed your experience.*

Use this four-step process to actively reframe your thinking about the stressful aspects of your workday.

> *First*, think about one of the most stress-inducing aspects of your workday.

> *Second*, reflect on what you have been telling yourself about this aspect of your workday. Have you been focusing on the negative by telling yourself things like: "This is awful because _____ ," or "this stresses me out because _____ ."

> *Third*, try to think of one positive thing about this aspect of your workday, no matter how small. This may take some mindful reflection, so allow yourself to pause and breathe deeply for at least three breaths.

> *Fourth*, change some small thing about what you do in how you interact with this aspect of your workday to amplify the one positive thing you identified above.

Now, use the Self-Care Graphic Organizer on the next page to begin your practice of reframing some of the unavoidable stressors in your workday. Changing how you think about stressful events, especially those you have little control over, can transform how you experience those events.

Cognitive Reframing to Manage Stress

Lightening your perception of stressors will reduce your body's overall stress response.

What is one of the most stressful aspects of my workday?

What have I been telling myself about this aspect of my day?

How can I think more positively about this to make it less stressful?

Are there any changes I can make based on my new way of thinking?

What is one of the most stressful aspects of my workday?

What have I been telling myself about this aspect of my day?

How can I think more positively about this to make it less stressful?

Are there any changes I can make based on my new way of thinking?

Cognitive Reframing to Manage Stress
(leave this page blank to make more copies as needed)

What is one of the most stressful aspects of my workday?	
What have I been telling myself about this aspect of my day?	
How can I think more positively about this to make it less stressful?	
Are there any changes I can make based on my new way of thinking?	

What is one of the most stressful aspects of my workday?	
What have I been telling myself about this aspect of my day?	
How can I think more positively about this to make it less stressful?	
Are there any changes I can make based on my new way of thinking?	

Pause and allow yourself a
few moments of quiet.

Grant Yourself A Day of Self-Care

Sometimes you need to take a whole day to intentionally pause your tasks, worries, and the needs of others to care for your wellbeing. It's an act of self-validation, grace, and self-love.

If you are a single parent, consider buddying up with another single parent to trade babysitting to grant each other a day of self-care. Also, consider taking a mental-health day off from work so you can care for yourself while your children are at school or daycare.

Here is one example of a full day of self-care:

1. *Begin with good bedtime habits to ensure that you get at least eight hours of sleep.*

2. *Wake up and take five to fifteen minutes for mindful reflection before jumping into activities.*

3. *Turn on some music, make your bed, and clear any clutter that may be in your bedroom.*

4. *Have a healthy breakfast.*

5. *Take a break from the gym and go outside for a walk or bike ride.*

6. *On your way home, observe your surroundings, and pay attention to the different types of people, plants, or animals.*

7. *Take a warm bath or hot shower, and then have a relaxing skincare routine.*

8. *Watch your favorite TV show or that one movie you haven't had time to watch.*

9. *Prepare or go to a coffee shop for a healthy lunch. Take a break from your phone while eating lunch.*

10. *If you need to pick up your children, get takeout on the way home so you don't have to cook.*

11. *Plan to have dinner with friends or family. If this is not possible, plan a call with a friend or family member.*

12. *Do something fun to end the evening with yourself or with your family. It could be singing, dancing, reading, painting, or writing.*

13. *End the day by going to bed early enough to ensure that you get at least eight hours of sleep.*

Detail your day of self-care on the next page.

My Full Day of Self-Care

My Full Day of Self-Care
(leave this page blank to make more copies as needed)

In a world full of doing, doing, doing, pause for moments to breathe and just *be.*

Your School's Collective-Care Journey

Throughout this guide, I have focused on the aspects of professional stress that are primarily under your control—your appraisal of and your reaction to the stressors you are exposed to. This is because you must first manage the things under your control to ensure that you will not sacrifice your health and wellbeing while trying to change the systems over which you have less power.

Professional stress results from the transaction between a demanding workplace (expectations of the district, school, families, students, and the culture of the school), your level of exposure to those stressors, the thoughts and emotions that are triggered (anxiety, depression, self-worth, and demoralization), and the personal and professional resources that you have to manage those stressors. This means that professional stress occurs when your knowledge of pedagogical strategies, toolbox of classroom management practices, time allotted for meeting students' educational needs, and collegial support are not enough to meet the challenges of your school or classroom. Simply put, the work is just too much more than you can handle.

Positive Stress	Tolerable Stress	Toxic Stress
Mild to moderate and short-lived stress exposure.	More severe stress exposure, limited in duration, with time and support for recovery.	Extreme, frequent, or extended stress exposure without the time and support for recovery.
Expectations and opportunities to complete tasks and work on projects that are just beyond your comfort zone of professional expertise.	Short-term deadlines that result in a time-limited increase in workload, and expectations to contribute to projects that require you to develop new competencies.	Pressured expectations that are too many or too far outside your professional expertise repeatedly trigger increase in stress hormones that create physiological and emotional distress.
Experiencing stress that motivates and energizes you to search out new learning and find creative solutions is personally and professionally healthy.	Experiencing stress that over activates your physiological stress responses is not harmful if there is enough time for your system to return to healthy levels before the next stressor, or if you receive professional support from colleagues.	Experiencing prolonged stress without relief or without professional support from colleagues is personally and professionally debilitating.

The goal is not the creation of a stress-free workplace where you never experience any challenges because experiencing professional stress just beyond your comfort zone fosters professional and personal growth. As shown in the figure above, professional stress becomes a problem when it lasts too long, and you don't receive adequate professional support to manage it.

> Too many districts and schools, through their policies and practices, create a workplace culture that intensifies stress and makes educators feel alone in their efforts to manage stress.

This closing section on collective-care focuses on the aspects of your workplace that can be changed by coming together as a collective of educators aiming to improve the system for yourselves and your students. Unfortunately, schools, especially those serving high numbers of low-income and racial and ethnic minority students, have high levels of student needs and insufficient human and material resources to meet those needs. Additionally, lower-income mostly minority schools are also where educators are subjected to intense pressures to increase student performance on standardized tests.

For classroom teachers, one of the ways that professional stress becomes toxic is when there are behaviorally dysregulated students in the classroom...

- **And** the teacher has exhausted their toolbox of classroom management strategies.
- **And** they see no improvement in the students' behaviors and likely an escalation in the frequency and severity of acting-out behaviors.
- **And** they feel pressured to increase time-on-task and improvements on standardized tests.
- **And** they don't have hope for improvement through professional development from their immediate colleagues or outside instructional coaching support.

This is an unnecessarily stressful professional context.

In this scenario, the classroom teacher is chronically stressed day after day, without relief. The stress does not decrease on weekends because they worry about the week to come. Keep in mind that this scenario leaves out many additional aspects of how school systems and individual schools are organized that make education a stressful profession. It is the accumulation of stressors that explains the high level of physical and emotional exhaustion—feeling worn out at the end of the school day and burnt out by the end of the academic year.

If you are one of these stressed educators, it is likely that your body is sending out physiological, psychological, and emotional warning signals that something is wrong and that your professional situation is demanding more of your than you have the capacity to manage. Unless you take corrective action to change the situation, the warning signals will develop into stress-induced diseases. Corrective action can occur through prevention, intervention, and remediation strategies.

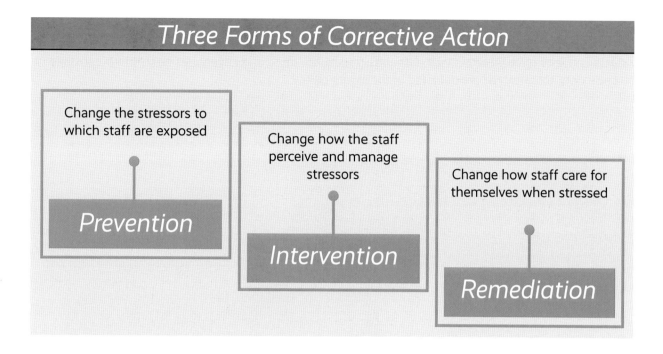

I will share three collective-care strategies, one for each form of corrective action:

1. **Prevention:** Collective examining of professional stressors and identifying opportunities for improvement
2. **Intervention:** Healing circles for professional social support
3. **Remediation:** Psychological First Aid from one educator to another

In most schools, the best strategy is to begin with intervention or remediation to strengthen collective staff wellbeing before attempting to change the core problem, which is minimizing and preventing the stressors to which staff are exposed.

Collective-care works at the intersection of the individual and the school by changing school systems that are beyond the control of any individual staff member while simultaneously building each individual's capacity to meet workplace demands. Teresa McIntyre and colleagues describe the positive cascade of outcomes that are depicted in the figure below.

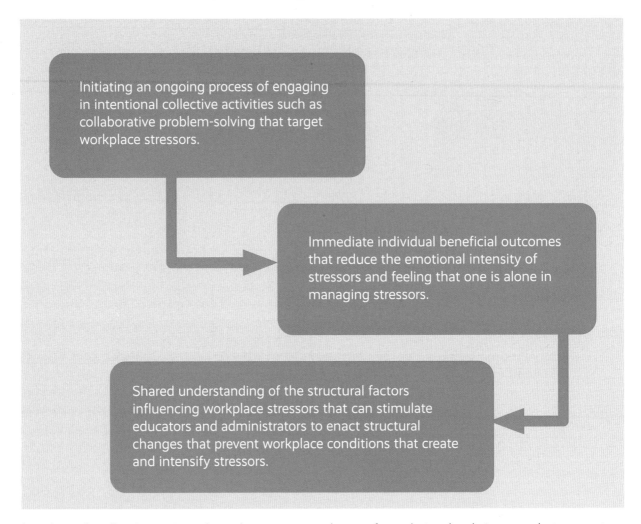

It is through collective actions that educators can truly transform their schools in ways that prevent stressors and increase the social support available in the building to manage stressors that cannot be eliminated. Collegial social support is much more than collective commiserating; it is providing emotional, informational, and instrumental support that is aimed at understanding, and managing, and eliminating stressors. Support from colleagues has proven to be stronger than support from family and friends because of the shared professional knowledge and understanding of the school context. The added benefit, shown in numerous research studies, is that student achievement increases as schools increase their level of trust among educators, between staff and principals, and overall collegial corporation.

PREVENTION: Collective Examination of Professional Stressors and Identifying Opportunities for Improvement

Gather a few colleagues who are ready to engage in the process of identifying and changing systemic factors that can reduce stress for all staff in your school. Review each of the five major categories of educator stress listed in the table beginning on the next page, and honestly reflect on what is happening at your school. Identify one to three small incremental changes that can create small but meaningful improvements.

We often want to start big, but a few small incremental changes are better than attempting to transform your school with one large change. Small changes can be initiated quickly, and as staff sees that change is possible, more will buy in, and motivation will build for making more significant changes.

It will be important for the group to move away from focusing on unhelpful questions about assigning blame for what is wrong to focusing on helpful questions about identifying the desired outcomes and the actions necessary to achieve those outcomes. This can be done with a solution-focused orientation to discussing problems. Once a problem has been identified, the goal is to move toward positive change by identifying the times and spaces in the school's history or present when the problem is much lessened. By identifying times and spaces when the problem is less severe or even absent, staff often discover that people in the school have already begun finding small solutions to the problem.

The **FORWARD** acronym developed by Coert Visser and Gwenda Schlundt Bodien is detailed on the next page to illustrate the solution-focused approach.

Moving FORWARD with a Solutions-Focused Approach to Problem-Solving	
Focus	Focus on what the team wants to be different. There may be something negative that you want to stop or there may be something positive you want to increase.
Outcomes	Describe the desired outcome in detail by focusing on specifying the concrete positive results of the changes the team desires. Once you collectively do this, the change process has actually begun.
Realized	Re-discover and describe what is already working well in the school, and from there find practical ideas to apply to making the desired change happen; learn from and use what has worked well to make progress.
When	Search for and identify exceptions to the problem: times when the current problem was less problematic or does not occur. When is the outcome you want to achieve already happening to some extent?
Action	Agree to take small steps forward instead of big leaps. Small steps do not require overcoming large motivational and trust barriers because if it does not work, not much will be lost, and if it works there is a chance of positive snowball effects.
Results	Monitor for and share any positive change. Noticing that you are moving forward is supportive to making further change and increases positive snowball effects.
Desire	Make desire for further change explicit by setting the next small collective goal and continuing to take small steps FORWARD.
You don't have to use all the steps every time; you may decide to leave out one or more steps when you apply the framework to a given problem.	

Review Potential Stressors and Identify Opportunities for Improvement

1. Organizational Structure Stressors		
Sources of Stress	**Assessment of school's stressors**	**One to three incremental change improvements**
Educators tend to have higher levels of stress in schools lacking: a supportive school culture, collaborative and collegial environment, trust among colleagues, strong principal leadership, and consistent leadership.		

2. Job Demand Stressors		
Sources of Stress	**Assessment of school's stressors**	**One to three incremental change improvements**
Stress of meeting the diverse and complex needs of students is often exacerbated by the continuously increasing workload, high-stakes testing, and other "accountability" pressures that may limit educator autonomy and threaten their jobs or the vitality of the school.		

Review Potential Stressors and Identify Opportunities for Improvement

3. Support and Autonomy Stressors		
Sources of Stress	**Assessment of school's stressors**	**One to three incremental change improvements**
Educators tend to have higher levels of stress in schools without adequate collegial support like mentoring for new educators, structured opportunities to observe and engage in peer learning, and opportunities to meaningfully contribute to school-level decisions.		

4. Interpersonal Stressors		
Sources of Stress	**Assessment of school's stressors**	**One to three incremental change improvements**
When educators themselves have weak social and emotional competencies, it can be difficult to manage the emotions that are triggered by challenging interactions with students, families, and colleagues; instruction often suffers and becomes another stressor.		

Review Potential Stressors and Identify Opportunities for Improvement

5. Behavior and Classroom Management Stressors

Sources of Stress	Assessment of our school's stressors	One to three incremental change improvements
Lack of knowledge and skills with managing emotional and behavioral challenges is often reported as the primary source of classroom stress. This includes acting out behaviors as well as internalizing behaviors such as disengagement and emotional withdrawal. Additionally, most educators have received limited professional training on child development, mental health, and trauma that would enable them to manage the increasing child and youth mental health crisis.		

INTERVENTION: Healing Circles for Professional Social Support

Healing circles allow educators to validate and manage the effects of stress collectively. This reduces feelings of self-blame and enables collective support in the healing process. A healing circle is an educator-led space where participants share their experiences and stories, affirm each other's resilience and voice, and work towards collective stress reduction.

Start small. Join with one or two colleagues who are on their own personal journey of reducing and managing professional stress. It only takes a few to start a healing circle at school.

Here is one suggestion for a healing circle meeting agenda to get you started.

Open with A Mindfulness Practice

- (Be sure the space is clean, welcoming, and comfortable)
- The circle keeper welcomes everyone to the circle and establishes it as a safe space.
- The circle keeper leads a brief mindfulness practice to center attention in the present moment.

Set the Intention

- The circle keeper states the purpose and hopes for the healing circle.
- The circle keeper reviews the pre-determined procedure for sharing. This is often done using a "talking piece" that each participant holds when they are ready to speak. All participants give attention to the person holding the talking piece.
- The circle keeper reviews additional pre-determined meeting agreements.

Engage in Collective-Care

- The circle keeper poses a question or offers a prompt to which participants can respond. Participants will share the talking piece as desired.
- The circle keeper poses a question or offers a prompt for a quiet reflection time for journaling followed by paired discussion.
- The circle keeper ends with a few words that express appreciation for what has been shared and highlights the importance of the overall work that has been done.

Close with A Mindfulness Practice

- The circle keeper leads a brief mindfulness practice to foster calm.

If the outcome of your healing circles is that you learn that staff wellbeing is so impaired that professional intervention is needed, work with your administrators to bring clinicians into the school for staff mental health support. A few courageous principals have invited a counselor or psychologist to provide mental health support during staff meetings, and all have stated that it is one of the best investments they have made in supporting staff wellbeing. These start as informational workshops and become more in-depth based on staff willingness to go further.

REMEDIATION: Psychological First Aid from One Educator to Another

Educators usually learn about Psychological First Aid as strategies for helping students cope with traumatic experiences, but it can also be used to help educators support each other through the stress of meeting students' needs. You can find many professional resources for learning the core components online by searching for "Psychological First Aid for Schools."

In the table below, the core components of Psychological First Aid have been adapted to illustrate how educators can provide each other with peer-to-peer psychological support.

1. Listen

Approach a fellow educator in distress and encourage them to share their feelings. It is important for educators to use active listening, validate their colleagues' feelings, and avoid fixing their problems.

2. Protect

Any staff member can experience secondary traumatic stress. Recognize and act on the importance of changing the school environment to reduce the risk of traumatization.

3. Connect

Because one common reaction to a traumatic event is emotional and social isolation, it is critical for educators to help each other maintain social relationships and create new ones.

4. Model Calm and Optimistic Behavior

Talk about school and life challenges in ways that focus on problem-solving and making small incremental improvements.

5. Learn

Learn how to identify stress symptoms and how and when to approach a colleague exhibiting signs of distress. This can be as simple as acknowledging to a peer that you see their distress and, when appropriate, that you have had similar experiences and feelings.

One of the most important ways that educators can engage in collective-care is by helping each other recognize when stress may be becoming toxic, normalizing the understanding that needing support to manage professional stress is not a sign of weakness, and being accountability partners through the active process of stress reduction and management.

People often need to receive permission and encouragement from colleagues to engage in work-related self-care.